Spotligh
Shakes

David Barr

Cassell Graded Readers Level 4

General Editor: Michael Carrier

Cassell
London

CASSELL LTD
35 Red Lion Square, London WC1R 4SG
an affiliate of
Macmillan Publishing Co. Inc.
New York

First published 1982

British Library Cataloguing in Publication Data

Barnaby, David
   Spotlight on Shakespeare. — (Cassell graded
   readers; level 4)
   1. English language — Text-books for foreigners
   2. Readers
   3. Shakespeare, William
   I. Title
   428.6'4   PE1128

ISBN 0-304-30597-9

Printed in Hong Kong by Wing King Tong Printing Co. Ltd.

Our thanks are due to the following for permission
to reproduce photographs:

The Mansell Collection (pp 20, 23, 40)
Morgan Wells (pp 30, 44, 45)

Contents

CASSELL GRADED READERS

ELEMENTARY

Spotlight on

Level 1
(350 headwords)

- A Doctor's Day
- Illusions
- Muhammad Ali
- A Radio Station

Level 2
(700 headwords)

- The Beginning of Radio
- Inventions
- British Food
- Tennis

INTERMEDIATE

Spotlight on

Level 3
(1050 headwords)

- Motor Racing
- Football
- The Kennedys
- The Common Market

Level 4
(1400 headwords)

- Surprises of Nature
- Fleet Street
- William Shakespeare
- Strange Stories

ADVANCED

Spotlight on

Level 5
(1750 headwords)

- British Theatre
- The Pop Industry

Level 6
(2100 headwords)

- The English Revolution
- Winston Churchill

Preface

This is a new series of readers for foreign students of English. It is new in several ways. Firstly, it has been designed as a series rather than an arbitrary group of titles. Secondly, the series provides reading material that is representative of the students' interests and corresponds as far as possible to the books that students would read in their own language. Thus it consists only of informative, entertaining, non-fiction topics. Thirdly, the language used in the readers has been carefully chosen and controlled so as to be easily understandable for students without being childish or patronising in its tone. At the same time each reader introduces a sizeable amount of subject-specific vocabulary which would not normally be included in a simple grading system. This subject-specific vocabulary is carefully explained through text, illustration or glossary so that the student can deal with topics in a more serious and informative way.

There are six levels, Level 1 being the simplest and Level 6 the most difficult. Each level introduces *circa* 350 new headwords and the length of each reader depends on its level (cf. list of titles at the beginning of this book).

The language is controlled lexically according to a

grading system, and subject-specific vocabulary is added where appropriate. There is also a structural grading which keeps syntactic complexity to a level that is comprehensible to the student. This operates mainly in Levels 1-4.

As one of the main aims of Cassell's Graded Readers is to stimulate the students' interest and motivation to read, the books are presented in a lively and interesting format and are well illustrated throughout. Each book also contains follow-up exercises and activities to give students the opportunity to take their interest in the topic, as well as in the language, further than a merely passive reading of the text.

Further details of the linguistic grading can be found in the Teachers' Guide to the series, obtainable from the publishers.

Colchester, 1982   Michael Carrier
                                          General Editor

1
Childhood in Stratford

In 1565 Stratford-on-Avon was a very busy place. It was one of the largest towns in Warwickshire, with a beautiful church called Holy Trinity and a fine bridge over the river Avon. London was only a hundred miles away and there were good roads which connected it with Stratford. Trade was good and there were plenty of opportunities*. Stratford was an attractive place for the young men who lived in the villages nearby who did not want to be farmers like their fathers.

John Shakespeare was one of the young men who came to Stratford to begin a new life. The trade he chose to learn was glovemaking* and, in time, he became very successful. He married a local girl called Mary Arden who came from a good family and he became an important person in the town. By 1565 John Shakespeare was an officer of the town and later he became the mayor (the most important member of the town government).

In 1558 John's first child, a girl, was born. It was a good year for England as well as for John Shakespeare because it was the year in which Elizabeth I became Queen of England. Although there were many political* and

---

* See *Glossary*.
  New words are asterisked (*) the first time they occur only.

religious* problems and England was not very friendly with Spain, English people were very hopeful about the future. It was the beginning of a great age.

In 1562 the Shakespeares had another baby daughter but unfortunately, she, like her elder sister, died soon after she was born. In 1564, John Shakespeare's luck returned: his first son was born. The records of Holy Trinity church in Stratford say that the baby was given the name William on 26th April 1564. There is no record of the exact day the baby was born but English people like to think that Shakespeare was born on 23rd April not only because he died on 23rd April 1616 but also because 23rd April is St George's Day. St George is the patron* saint* of England.

The year in which William was born was a year of plague* in the town and John Shakespeare knew that he

Stratford in the 16th century

was lucky that his baby son had lived through the dangerous early months of life. The plague was a terrible illness; it was very common in England and the rest of Europe at that time but nobody knew that the plague was carried by rats (small animals like mice but bigger and more dangerous). People thought that the plague was a punishment* from God — so the rats continued to live and the plague continued to spread.

In the same year as William, another small boy was born in Canterbury, about 150 miles away from Stratford. His father was a shoemaker and his name was Christopher Marlowe. He too, was going to become a famous playwright*. English drama*, as well as John Shakespeare, could look forward to a bright future.

There had been plays* in England for several hundred years. The people of Stratford, as in many other towns, enjoyed drama from time to time. Sometimes the church services had some drama in them, especially the services at Christmas and Easter. The priests (men of the church) would act* for the people because all the services were in Latin, which most people did not understand. If they could see real people speaking and acting scenes from Christ's life then they could understand and remember them more easily.

For hundreds of years English people had been able to watch religious plays. They were often acted in groups, each play telling one part of a long story from the Bible. It was a custom for a lot of these plays to be acted out one after the other on the day of Corpus Christi at Easter time.

The people also saw morality* plays, which were not religious but were sometimes acted by professional* actors* who travelled from town to town. The characters in the play were not like real people, but more like good or bad qualities* in human form. They had names like 'wisdom*', 'pleasure' and 'foolishness'. Even though the characters were not like real people, these plays were very popular with the people of Stratford. They showed the happiness and sadness of their own lives in a way they could understand. It helped them to see their problems acted out by other people and it gave them comfort.

There was a lot of violent* physical action in the morality plays and the audience* was often just as violent. They did not sit and watch quietly as audiences do today but they cried if the play was tragic (sad) or shouted with laughter if the play was comic (funny).

Religious plays and morality plays were not taken very seriously by the educated people of the time. They believed that all the best plays had been written by the Greek and Roman* writers of the earlier times. They thought that the best any English writer could do was to write good copies of these older plays. But at the time that William was born, ideas about the theatre and about the English language were just beginning to change: three years before Shakespeare was born, a play called *Gorboduc* was performed for the queen. The form of the play was copied from a Roman play, but it was still a good play. The most important thing was that it was written in English. This performance* reminds us of two other signs that England was nearly ready for a playwright such as William Shakespeare: firstly, educated English people were beginning to realise that their own language might be just as suitable for education*, books and the law* as it was for farming, shopping and the home; and secondly, Queen Elizabeth herself was very fond of the theatre.

By 1568 William was four years old and was beginning to notice life in Stratford. In that year this father was chosen as mayor (the most important man) of the town. William was old enough to be happy for his father when he appeared in his mayor's clothes with all the other important people of the town.

In the next year a group of professional actors visited Stratford and the town gave them a big welcome. William's father, because he was the mayor, helped to welcome them and the Earl* of Worcester's men performed their plays in the town. This was five-year-old William's first experience of English drama.

It was in these early years that the young William Shakespeare caught the feeling of excitement that the travelling actors brought with them. Perhaps he watched the play from his father's knee — they certainly had a good view because Will's father was an important man in the town. Will loved the bright colours, the costumes* and the scenery* and especially the scene at the end of one of the morality plays when the hero (the most important actor) was changed into a pig! Drama was exciting and yet it was part of everyday life in Stratford; the different groups of actors came and went every year like the seasons. People did not go to the theatre as they do today (there were no buildings called 'theatres'), but the theatre came to them. The seeds* of Shakespeare's love for the theatre were sown* in those days and, as we know, the fruit* was very very good.

2
Schooldays

No one can be sure how long William's schooldays lasted. In fact, no one is sure where he went to school, although most people agree that he probably went to Stratford Grammar School, which offered free education to sons of full citizens* of Stratford, such as John Shakespeare.

In the sixteenth century*, boys usually went to school between the ages of seven and thirteen. First, they went to an elementary* school. Here they practised reading and writing in English. Later, the boys went to a grammar* school. Grammar schools were called 'grammar' schools, not because they taught English grammar, but because they taught Latin grammar. In fact, the main purpose of a grammar school was to teach Latin. For most people at this time, education meant learning Latin because there were very few books written in English. The works of Geoffrey Chaucer (a writer of the fourteenth century, who wrote in English) were not understood by most people, and the Bible alone was not enough. The English language had a great future, but for the eleven-year-old boys at grammar school all the lessons were in Latin.

The fact that Shakespeare did not learn English

grammar may have been a good thing. When he later came to write for the theatre, he did not feel that he had to follow any rules about the language. This is why Shakespeare's language is so free and unusual. He was not afraid of changing the English language and if he could not find a suitable word for a speech he would make a new one. It is thanks to him that the English language is so rich today.

Let us look at three other children in the year when William was eleven years old, who all knew him as an adult. There was a three-year-old boy in Westminster who was the son of a builder. He is better known as the playwright Ben Jonson. There was a five-year-old girl in London who was the daughter of one of the queen's musicians*. In later years she and William became very good friends. William often wrote about her in his poems although he never gave her name — which was Emilia Bassano. She is known as 'the dark lady' because she is always described in the sonnets as having dark hair, dark eyes and dark skin. The third child who was later to know Shakespeare was a child called Henry Wriothesley, who was two years old at this time. He later became the third Earl of Southampton and he, too, played an important part in William's later life.

Queen Elizabeth I liked drama — she herself was quite a dramatic character. She had a difficult job being the monarch* at that time. Political problems and religious problems were much the same thing in Elizabethan England. As queen, Elizabeth was head of the Protestant (non-Catholic) Church of England. As far as possible, she

Queen Elizabeth I

was a tolerant* queen, but she had to protect* herself against the Catholics who wanted a Catholic monarch. She also had problems with the Puritans (extreme Protestants) who, amongst other things, were against the theatre and most kinds of public entertainment. They did not like the idea of large groups of people coming together to enjoy themselves because this could lead to the spread of Catholic ideas.

There were Puritans in the governments of many towns and cities, including London. They were powerful enough to make life difficult for anyone who earned his living by writing plays or by acting: in 1572 the Mayor of London had forbidden all performances by actors inside the city walls. Plays and other entertainments (such as bull-baiting* and bear-baiting) all took place in the parts of London which were outside the city walls. Two years later, London actors who were not protected by a powerful person (such as the Earl of Worcester) were not allowed to perform in other towns. Of course, the queen's power was great, and wherever she was, there were plays and actors.

In 1576, when William was twelve years old, a man called James Burbage built the first proper theatre in London. It was called simply The Theatre. Naturally, it was not inside the city walls — the Puritans made sure of that. Burbage was a good businessman and he saw that the performance of plays could bring him a lot of money in the future. He loved plays himself, but he also wanted to get back the money that he had spent on building the theatre. For this reason he built a big theatre so that everyone who wanted to see a play there would be able to get in. He wanted the theatre to be for the ordinary people as much as for the rich.

Before The Theatre was built, plays were performed in the courtyards* of inns (drinking houses). The owners* of the inns were quite happy about this because it meant that people would spend more money on drink and food. Most people stood in the courtyard to watch the play, while the rich lords and ladies sat in the balcony* of the inn, on the first floor. (If you go to a theatre in England today, you will find that the seats on the first floor are still called 'balcony' seats.)

There were no newspapers in those days, so news travelled more slowly than it does today. The great meeting place in London for the exchange of news and talk as well as goods (food etc.), was St Paul's Cathedral. The people who sold food and other things from foreign countries stopped at St Paul's as soon as they arrived in London — they could bring their ships all the way up the River Thames in those days. Religion and politics had a great effect on the everyday life of the people, who were becoming more and more interested in what was going on in other countries as people travelled further and further.

In 1572 hundreds of Protestants were killed in France on St Bartholomew's Day. The English were very frightened. The difference between the Catholics and Protestants was becoming greater.

In 1577 Francis Drake, one of the queen's sailors, left England to go on a long journey by sea. He returned three years later after sailing round the world. He was the first man to do this since Magellan's men in 1522. Drake became famous because he was successful in stealing large amounts of gold from Spanish ships and bringing it back to England. This caused bad feeling between England and Spain and it did not help the situation between the Catholics and the Protestants in England. The English Protestants thought that the Spanish (who were Catholics) would help the English Catholics to remove Queen Elizabeth and have a Catholic monarch instead of her.

These were times of change and excitement. English people were beginning to be influenced by Europe, especially Italy. It was very fashionable* to ride in the Italian way, the English started to build houses in the Italian style*, and when poets wrote love songs they copied an Italian poet called Petrarch. Literature* was beginning to grow better and better: Spenser had written some beautiful poetry, North had made good English translations* of foreign books. The first theatre was built and Drake had sailed round the world.

For William Shakespeare's father, however, the future was not quite so exciting. For some reason that we do not know, John Shakespeare began to stay away from meetings of the town's officers during William's school years. He owed money and he had to sell some of his wife's property* so that he could get the money. He started to play a less important part in public life. A few years later, all his public responsibility was taken from him. He even had to pay £20, with 140 other men, for not going to church and town meetings. John was a sad man. Family life became less pleasant; these were difficult times for the Shakespeare family.

3
The missing years

The years between Shakespeare's life as a schoolboy in Stratford and his life as a playwright in London are often called 'the missing years'. Very little is known about him during this time, but we do know that by 1585 he was a married man with a two-year-old daughter and newly-born twins*.

Let us fill in the missing five or six years as well as we can. From about 1579 Shakespeare's family had bad luck. In addition to John Shakespeare's own misfortune*, William's seven-year-old sister died in 1579. Perhaps William went to school until he was thirteen, or perhaps he left school earlier in order to help the family by earning some money. Some people believe he was a teacher for some time; others think he was a soldier, or that he worked in a lawyer's* office. Perhaps all three are true; perhaps none are.

We do not know how many girl friends there were in the life of the young Shakespeare, but there were at least two. Both were called Anne. Some people say that Shakespeare planned to marry Anne Whateley, but he married Anne Hathaway instead. Anne Hathaway was eight years older than William. She and William were married in 1582 and their daughter, Susanna, was born

Anne Hathaway's cottage

six months later.

William and Anne probably went to live in Stratford with the Shakespeare family. In 1585 there were eleven people in the house so it must have been crowded and difficult, especially since William found that he did not get on very well with his new wife. He felt unhappy. He did not want his future to be like his father's. He was still only 21 years old and was not ready to begin married life. He wanted to go to London and see life. . .

In 1587 five companies of actors visited Stratford. Among them were the Queen's Men and the Earl of Leicester's Men. At some time during this year, Shakespeare left Stratford and went to live in London. His first wish was to become an actor. It was only later that he started to write plays (and poetry*) because there was not much good material to use in the theatre. Shakespeare probably changed many plays that were performed by his company. Shakespeare learnt how to write plays at the same time as he was learning how to act but, for him, writing came second to acting. Not all the actors in a company needed to be able to write plays but they all needed to know how to act, sing, dance, play musical instruments* and fight with swords*. For several years Shakespeare learnt how to act the hard way — and there was a lot to learn. He was also learning a lot about the theatre at the same time and finding out what sort of plays the audiences liked.

The playwrights of this time were all university* men, not professional actors like Shakespeare. In the early 1580s the plays of these university men (Christopher Marlowe was one of them) were probably the best plays of the time. But as the professional actors and the theatres grew better, the theatre people wrote their own plays more and more. The plays made from the Latin and Greek stories, which the university men wrote, were no longer popular. The audiences wanted something closer to their everyday lives. Christopher Marlowe wrote the plays which brought together the university men and the professional actors most successfully. In 1587, when Shakespeare went to London, Marlowe's play *Tamburlaine the Great* was performed. It told the story of an ordinary shepherd who became a powerful and cruel king. The language was violent and beautiful and it influenced Shakespeare's own writing.

The plays of the time (like *Tamburlaine the Great* by Christopher Marlowe and *The Spanish Tragedy* by Thomas Kyd) often included lots of blood, violence* and

ghosts. They were like real life at that time. The torture*
of animals for entertainment and of men for public
punishment were common in those days. Mary Stuart,
whom the Catholics wanted to be queen, had her head
cut off in 1587.

The feeling between Catholics and Protestants in
England got worse as the feeling between Protestant
England and Catholic Spain got worse. However, as war
became a possibility, the English began to think more
about their own country. A man called Holinshed (whom
Shakespeare may have met in Warwickshire) wrote the
first book in English about the history of England. It was
very popular because it came just at the time when the
English were beginning to feel patriotic*. They wanted to
know more about their country's history because they
were glad to be English. Shakespeare did not take long to
use this general feeling in his writing: when he took his
facts for a new play called *Harry VI* from Holinshed's
book, he knew that it was sure to be successful. In fact, it
was so successful that he decided to write more history
plays so that the audience could follow the history of their
country from Richard II right through to Henry VIII who
was the father of their queen, Elizabeth I.

In the history about Henry IV, the audiences were
introduced to the character of Falstaff, who became the
most famous comic character in English literature.

Meanwhile, the patriotism of the English was tested.
In 1588, the King of Spain sent many ships to attack
England. The English were not afraid — especially with a
brave queen like Elizabeth to lead them. She told them:
'I know I have the body of a weak woman, but I have the

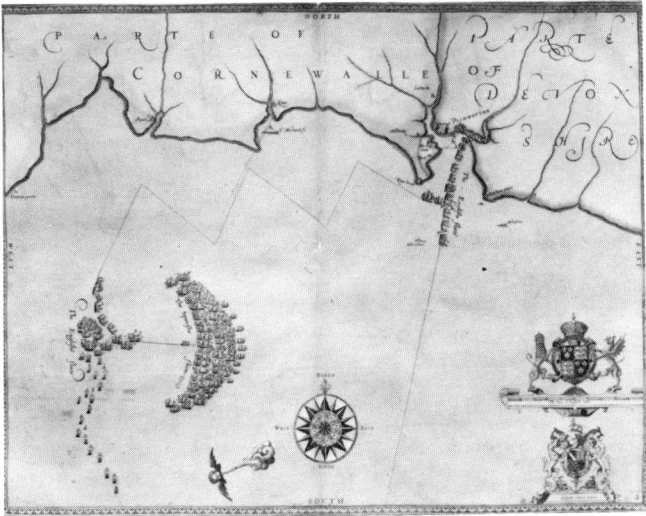

The Spanish armada

heart and stomach of a king.'

The Spanish ships were very big and carried thousands of soldiers. The smaller, faster English ships met the big Spanish ships in the English Channel, where the water was quite rough. The Spanish soldiers never landed in England because they fought at sea and the Spanish fleet was broken up. One of the English leaders was the famous Francis Drake who had stolen gold from the Spanish ships so bravely some years before.

It was a great year for the English, and a great year for Shakespeare to be in London. The exciting things that were happening abroad had an effect on the people in England which meant that the theatre also felt a change. The time was just right for the growth of Shakespeare's genius*.

4
Early years in London

When the Queen's Men visited Stratford in 1587 they were without one of their actors. It is possible that Shakespeare took the place of the missing man, and this is why he left Stratford at that time. In any case, he probably worked as an actor and as a writer with the Queen's Men (a group of actors who were helped by the queen) during his early years in London — the years that we know so little about. When he left the Queen's Men and joined Lord Strange's Men (a group of actors who were helped by Lord Strange), however, his career began to show signs of success. Lord Strange's Men were a very good acting group and they had already performed several times for the queen. They were very fortunate to have as their chief actor Edward Alleyn, who was one of the best-known actors of the time.

London was a very exciting place for a young man at this time: people were no longer happy to keep to the old rules of society, they felt a new sense of freedom and opportunity. Business and trade were going very well. People had more money than before and they were able to use it to build and to travel.

An actor-manager (the name for a man who is an actor

as well as a businessman in the theatre) called Philip Henslowe had spent a large amount of money on rebuilding a theatre called The Rose and Lord Strange's Men performed some plays there in 1592. The Rose, of course, was outside the London city walls because they were still many Puritans in power inside the city who refused to give permission for theatres to be built. Henslowe watched the sizes of the audiences very carefully. Two plays by Robert Greene (one of the university men) did not get large audiences but the theatre was full for a play by Christopher Marlowe called *The Jew of Malta*. Marlowe was the same age as Shakespeare but his talent* for writing plays had grown earlier than Shakespeare's. *The Jew of Malta* was not his first successful play; he was already known as the writer of *Doctor Faustus* and *Tamburlaine the Great*.

After *The Jew of Malta*, the next play at The Rose was Shakespeare's first history play, *Henry VI*. It was the most successful play of the season. The only person who was not very pleased was Robert Greene, the university man. He was very angry that a simple actor from outside London who did not even have a university education had written a play which was more popular than his.

It is clear that Shakespeare the writer had been watching the audiences as carefully as Henslowe the businessman. William was much more in touch with the audiences than any of the university men because he was like them. He was the same as the people who came to watch the plays who laughed and cried and shouted. He know what the audiences wanted to see and he knew what the actors wanted to act. He was in the best place to write for the theatre.

Plays about English history, English kings and European wars were what interested the public at this time. The English had only recently experienced the new, exciting feeling of patriotism. This feeling had reached its peak in 1588 when a group of small English ships destroyed the big Spanish ships completely. History plays helped the people to re-live their recent experience — they could feel again the same pride* in their country.

Shakespeare wrote a play called *Titus Andronicus* at about this time. It is a play that is so full of horror* that many people today find it difficult to watch. When it was shown in London recently some people walked out and one lady fainted! (She fell down.) The next play Shakespeare wrote was called *The Comedy of Errors*. It was taken from an old story about the mixed identities* of twins. (Shakespeare's own twins, Hamnet and Judith, were seven or eight years old when the play was written.) This is light and amusing and very different to *Titus Andronicus*. Perhaps the fact that Shakespeare could write two such different plays at about the same time shows that he was writing to please his audience rather than to please himself. When he later came to write the tragedies he did not write any comedies at the same time but wrote only about these serious subjects.

In 1592 and 1593 the plague was very bad in London. When the plague was at its worst, the theatres and other places of public entertainment* were closed down so the Puritans were pleased. They thought that the plague was

God's punishment for theatres and happiness of that sort. Many plays of the time, such as *The Spanish Tragedy*, *Titus Andronicus* and (the most famous of all) *Hamlet*, were about punishment. In 1593 the plague killed a thousand people in London every week and the theatres remained closed. This was a good chance for the actors to perform in other towns, and perhaps to visit Stratford.

Shakespeare's plays at this time (*Titus Andronicus* for instance) showed that he knew how to write plays with good 'box-office' value — that is, that attracted a lot of people. Violence and punishment were both common in those days and if the people wanted to see violence, punishment and horror on the stage — and were willing to pay for it — then Shakespeare was willing to write it for them. These early plays were very popular but Shakespeare felt that he could do greater things.

At that time people thought that playwriting was not very respectable*. The plays, once they were written, did not belong to the writers but to the company (group of actors) who acted them. So, the play *Henry VI* belonged not to Shakespeare but to Lord Strange's company. Any printer* who could get a copy could print it without paying the author anything.

Shakespeare realised that to be a famous writer and to make some money he would have to write poetry as well as plays. In 1591, when he was in London, but still unknown, he read some fourteen line poems* called sonnets written by a well-known writer called Philip Sidney. Educated people liked Sidney's ideas and many copied him and wrote sonnets of their own. A writer could be more personal, both about himself and about his friends, when writing sonnets. These poems were sometimes printed, but more often copied by hand and passed among friends. Around 1592 Shakespeare began to write sonnets for wealthy people as well as plays for the acting companies.

In the same year Robert Greene died. He died an unhappy man, a half-successful playwright with no money. In order to make as much money as possible some of his friends took all his papers to a printer. One of his pieces of writing was against non-university people like Shakespeare who were more successful as playwrights than university men like himself. He made a joke about Shakespeare's name (he called him 'Shake-scene') and included a line from one of Shakespeare's plays. What he said was so unkind that Shakespeare went to see the printer, who said he was sorry. Greene's attack tells us how successful Shakespeare was, even in 1592.

When Greene died, it was a sad day for the theatre. Only a short time before, Christopher Marlowe had written a new history play, and his death*, the following year, was another great loss* to the theatre. He did not die peacefully in his bed like Greene; he was killed with a knife in the head during a fight at an inn. Some people believe that Marlowe was a spy* as well as a playwright, and that he was killed by people working for Spain.

The way was now clear for Shakespeare who went on to write *Love's Labour's Lost* and *The Taming of the Shrew* which were both comedies*; *Richard III*, another history play; more sonnets; and a long poem called *Venus and Adonis* which was printed and published*. This was the difference between poetry and plays — poetry was published, plays were not. The man who printed *Venus and Adonis* was called Robert Field. His home-town was Stratford. He had known William since he was a boy, and, like him, he had come to London to make his fortune — in other words — to get rich.

The book of *Venus and Adonis* contained a dedication (a few kind words) to Henry Wriothesley, Earl of Southampton, who gave Shakespeare help and protection. Shakespeare could not have written all he did without the help of this wealthy man. The poem itself is about an older goddess who tried to make a younger man love her. Shakespeare knew all about that because he had married a woman eight years older than himself.

Thomas Kyd, the writer of *A Spanish Tragedy*, died at about this time and Shakespeare became the chief playwright of London. He wrote two plays for the company which are now among his most famous: *A Midsummer Night's Dream*, which is a beautiful mixture of old English stories and Greek names and *Romeo and Juliet*, a romantic story told by many writers before Shakespeare but never as well as in this play.

The public theatres had been closed for over a year because of the plague and the Puritans. When they were opened again in 1594 there were some changes in the acting companies. Edward Alleyn went to join a new company — the Lord Admiral's Men at Henslowe's Rose Theatre (Alleyn was married to Henslowe's daughter),

while Shakespeare, Richard Burbage and others formed a
new company called the Lord Chamberlain's Men. They
performed in The Theatre, which had been built by
Richard Burbage's father, James Burbage.

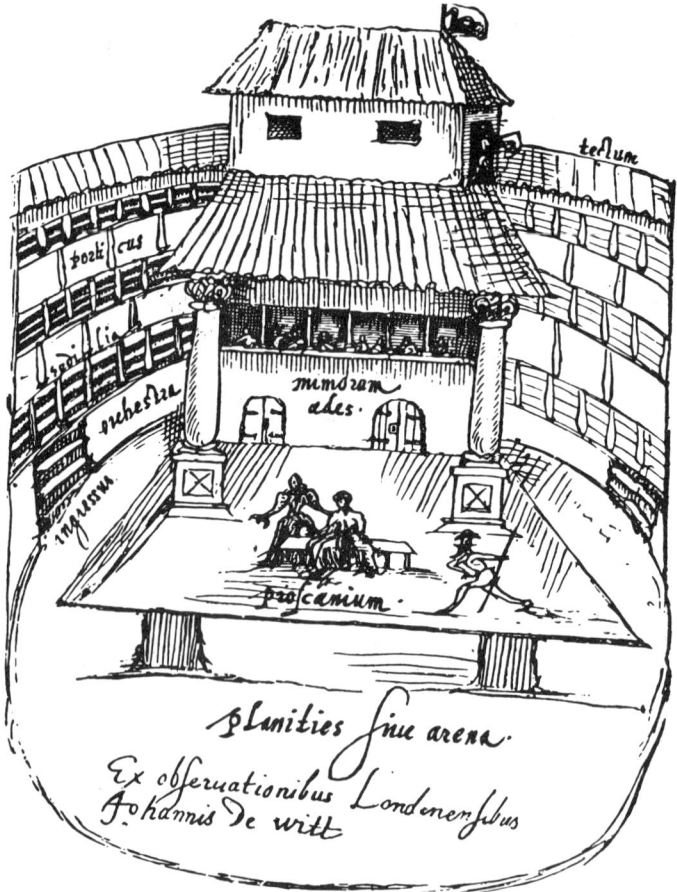

The Swan Theatre

If we look at Shakespeare's situation in 1595, we could not do better than use the words of Anthony Burgess: 'The Lord Chamberlain's Men, the greatest body of actors of all time, with the greatest playwright of all time, were at last in existence.' In that year Shakespeare wrote the play *Richard II*, and a fourth theatre was built in London. This theatre, The Swan, held three thousand people. Drama was now a real part of London life, in spite* of the Puritans.

Shakespeare stopped writing sonnets at about this time. He had written more than one hundred and fifty. They are all separate short poems, but together they tell a story. Many of them are addressed to a beautiful young man, to whom Shakespeare wrote with a mixture of admiration*, gratitude* and duty*. The man was Henry Wriothesley, the Earl of Southampton, Shakespeare's patron (helper) and friend. The sonnets also speak of a 'dark lady' whom Shakespeare loved but who liked someone else better (the Earl of Southampton himself). Students still argue about who this 'dark lady' was but most think she was Emilia Bassana, a daughter of one of the Queen's musicians. There was a triangle* of love, with the Earl, the 'dark lady' and Shakespeare at each of the corners. Although he had stopped writing sonnets, Shakespeare did not stop writing plays — he completed two plays about Henry IV and one about Henry V to add to his group of English history plays; a comedy set in Italy, about prejudice and love, called *The Merchant of Venice*; two more comedies called *Much Ado about Nothing* and *As You Like It* and another history, this time set in ancient* Rome, called *Julius Caesar*.

New Place

William Shakespeare was now a successful and prosperous man. Life was very good for him; but there was sadness as well as happiness in his life: his only son, Hamnet, died at the age of eleven. At about the same time, John Shakespeare had some good news for a change: he received a coat * of arms for his family (almost certainly with his son's help) and he could now call himself a 'gentleman' at last. Later, after his father's death William Shakespeare bought the second biggest house in Stratford; it was called New Place.

Shakespeare continued to write new plays in London and to meet interesting and clever people in the inns and coffee houses. In 1598 he met Ben Jonson for the first time when he acted in the first performance in London of

Jonson's play, *Everyman in his Humour*. Ben Jonson was a noisy, friendly man and he led a colourful life compared to the quiet courteous William Shakespeare. He drank a lot, had been in prison* once or twice, and had killed a man in a fight. Nevertheless, he and Shakespeare remained friends for many years.

At about this time there was some bad news for The Theatre and for the Burbage brothers (the sons of James Burbage who had built The Theatre in 1576 — which was the first theatre in London). The man who owned the land where The Theatre stood told the actors that they could no longer use his land — he had only leased it to them for a certain amount of time. The Burbages and their friends were not afraid: they simply took the old theatre, piece by piece, across the frozen* river Thames and built a new theatre on the other side. They called it The Globe, and it became the most famous of all the Elizabethan theatres. Like the other theatres, it was round. It stood for thirteen years until it burned* down. The fire was started by a spark from a gun which was used in the play. While the audience was escaping, a man's trousers caught fire and he was only saved because someone quickly poured a bottle of beer over him!

5
The successful playwright

By the time the seventeenth century arrived, things had changed. Shakespeare was a middle-aged man. He had achieved wealth and fame but the excitement and hope of the early years of his career had gone. He had experienced personal tragedy: his son Hamnet and several friends (including Christopher Marlowe) had died. He now looked at the world with the eyes of a man who had seen many things. His later writing showed that he had become more interested in the serious side of life than in comedy or romance.

Shakespeare's first play of the new century was a long tragedy or romance called *Hamlet, Prince of Denmark*. Hamlet is perhaps the best known of all Shakespeare's tragic characters and many actors have played the part in many different ways.

Shakespeare's tragedies were in some ways like the old plays of violence and cruelty written by Marlowe and Kyd. There is war and cruelty in all of them and many good people suffer and die. There are also short moments of laughter and fun but there is much more sadness and horror in these later tragedies than in the earlier histories, romances* and comedies.

The stories of the tragedies are often about the downfall* and death of a great man. The struggles* in the play happen in the man's mind rather than on the field of battle and the characters are often not what they seem. These are not simple plays and so the audience has to watch carefully and think a lot. The great man in the play always seems to bring about his downfall, and yet, at the same time, his downfall is not his own choice*. Each great man seems to see the world much more clearly after he has suffered.

Shakespeare wrote nearly a dozen tragedies, but modern students think that there are four 'great' tragedies: *Hamlet*, *Othello*, *King Lear*, and *Macbeth*. Othello is an African, the action is in Italy and Cyprus, and the questions in the play are universal — that is, they are true for everyone at all times. They are: jealousy (when we hate someone because we think they are better than we are) and ambition or greed (when we only think about ourselves and will do anything to get what we want in life — whether a good job or possessions). The stories of King Lear, a king of England, and Macbeth, a king of Scotland were told by Holinshed first but Shakespeare's plays are not just history plays. They are plays about men and, because Shakespeare showed these men so truthfully and with such understanding, they are also plays about all mankind.

The new king, after Queen Elizabeth I, who died in 1603, had been known as James VI of Scotland. He came to England to be James I of England and Scotland. It was lucky for the actors and playwrights that the new king liked plays. In fact, there were even more performances at court* than during Queen Elizabeth's time and the King made life very comfortable for Shakespeare's company. The Lord Chamberlain's Men became the King's Men and Shakespeare and the others had positions at the Court. They even had places in the church when the King was crowned. Later, King James let the Earl of Southampton out of prison.

It is possibly because the new king came from Scotland that Shakespeare chose a story about Scotland for a play he wrote in about 1605 called *Macbeth*. After *Hamlet*, the other three great tragedies were written quickly, one after the other, between 1604 and 1606.

We must not forget two comedies which remind us of the 1590s. One of these plays again had the popular character of Falstaff in it. There is a story that Queen Elizabeth I liked Falstaff so much that she wanted to see a play in which he was in love. The *Merry Wives of Windsor* was Shakespeare's answer to the Queen's wish. The play was written quickly and most people do not find the Falstaff of *The Merry Wives of Windsor* as funny as the Falstaff of the history plays. The other play was called *Twelfth Night*. It is a play in which twins had mixed-up identities. (Two of Shakespeare's own children were twins — Hamnet and Judith). This play is still very popular today.

Like Francis Drake (the man who had led the British ships to victory* against the Spanish Armada), the Earl of Essex was a popular military* leader. He was admired especially by Shakespeare's old friend, the Earl of Southampton. Essex had been a successful soldier during

The Globe Theatre

the reign of Queen Elizabeth I but when he was on his last job in Ireland he told the Irish rebels to wait because the queen would soon die and there would be a new government. Naturally, the queen was not pleased with him when he returned and he was punished. Both Essex and Southampton believed strongly that there should be a new king or queen.

They say that artists should watch life, not take part in it but on 7th February 1601 Shakespeare's company played a part in a political matter which did no-one any good. Shakespeare had never wanted to be involved in politics but this time he had no choice. A group of Essex's important friends came to The Globe on 6th February and paid a lot of money for a special performance of *Richard II* on the following day. They wanted to see this history play so quickly because it tells how a king is removed from his position and how his place is taken by one of his men. Essex's men wanted this play to be the first part of a rebellion* in which the queen was removed from the throne*. Shakespeare and the Burbages could not say no, so the play was performed. The rebellion did take place but it was not successful. Essex was taken prisoner and his head was cut off on 25th February 1601. The Earl of Southampton remained in prison until James I released him after the queen's death, two years later.

On 24th February the Lord Chamberlain's Men were called to perform a play for the queen. They were very afraid. One of the actors had to explain why the company had performed *Richard II* the day before the rebellion. The actors felt they were acting for their lives. Luckily, nothing happened to them, but the story shows how important drama had become. Twenty-five years before, no actors or play could change political life in any way.

In the same year, 1601, Shakespeare's father died in Stratford. After twenty years of bad luck, life was happier for him. He was a gentleman and he was once again a member of the Stratford council After his father's death, Shakespeare bought some land in Stratford. He now owned New Place, even though he worked in London.

While the queen was alive, Shakespeare wrote two

more plays, *Troilus and Cressida* and *All's Well that Ends Well*. The queen died peacefully on 24th March 1603; she had been queen for forty-four years. She had walked very carefully between Protestants and Catholics and so had brought years of peace, both inside and outside England. Business, art and beauty were able to grow as never before. During her last fifteen years, English drama had grown into a powerful and great literature*.

Shakespeare and Ben Jonson were now the best-known playwrights of the time. Shakespeare was writing a play about justice*. It was half tragedy and half comedy and was called *Measure for Measure*. Ben Jonson had had one or two plays in the London theatres but he became very good at writing masques, which James I enjoyed very much. Masques were expensive colourful mixtures of dance and drama and were always performed indoors*.

James I was not tolerant of Catholics. He persecuted* them cruelly. One group of men was so disappointed and angry about this violence that they planned to kill King James and most of his Protestant government. The leader of the group was a man called Robert Catesby, whose family had property in Stratford. They planned to explode* the Parliament buildings when King James, his family and his government were inside. Some Catholics would be in the buildings too, and this may be why the plan was discovered. Catesby and his men received a cruel punishment which made the Catholic-Protestant problem even worse.

Ben Jonson and Shakespeare knew most of the men involved in the plan, but today, most English people

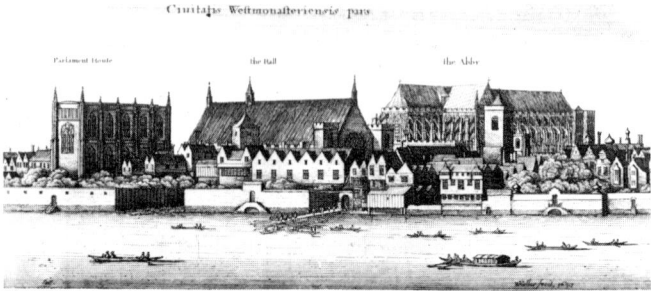

The Houses of Parliament in the 17th century

remember the name of only one of Catesby's men: Guy Fawkes. English people still remember this day every year on November 5th. They make a model of Guy Fawkes from paper and then burn it on the top of a big fire. Most people cannot remember whether Guy Fawkes was Catholic or Protestant — they just enjoy the fire and the fun!

In the year of the Gunpowder Plot, as it is now known, Shakespeare bought more property in Stratford. Clearly, he was planning to return there one day. His daughter, Susanna, married a Stratford doctor called John Hall in 1607. In the same year Shakespeare's mother died. The following year Susanna had a baby daughter, but there was another death in the family. Edmund, William's youngest brother, who was twenty-seven years old and also an actor, died in London. It must have seemed to Shakespeare that every good thing in life came at the same time as something bad.

Shakespeare was still writing at great speed: translations of Latin stories gave him some of the ideas for more tragedies. *Anthony and Cleopatra*, *Coriolanus* and *Timon of Athens* were all written around 1608. That year the plague came to London again and the King's Men began to use a second theatre further out of the city at Blackfriars although they still had lots of work at The Globe. For many years the Blackfriars Theatre had been the theatre of the childrens' acting companies. It belonged to the Burbages, but they had not used it until now. It was unusual because it was not round, it was indoors, and the stage* was at one end of a long room. It needed a different kind of acting and different kinds of audiences.

In 1609 a man called Thorpe published all Shakespeare's sonnets and a poem called *A Lover's Complaint* in one book. The sonnets were certainly by Shakespeare; the poem may be his, too. If so, he had written it many years before. The book sold many copies but people at that time were more interested in a ship called the *Sea Venture* which went down into the Atlantic on its way to the new world of Virginia. The people who were still alive found a group of beautiful islands filled with cedar trees and completely empty of people. Today we call the islands Bermuda.

Shakespeare talked, listened and wondered like everyone else but at the same time his playwright's mind* was working. First of all, however, he had to finish *Pericles, Prince of Tyre* and start to write *Cymbeline*. These two plays were neither happy like the early comedies nor sad like the tragedies. We call them 'romances'; they are peaceful and magical*, and the problems in them usually end happily. They were written to be performed in the Blackfriars Theatre which was indoors so the language is much quieter. The actors did not have to shout to be heard by the audience who could all sit down to watch the play. Because the shape of the stage was now square and not round, there were more opportunites to make special and unusual scenery. Shakespeare and other playwrights changed their plays to suit the new building so that they were less 'wordy' and more visual * — in other words it was as important to feel the atmosphere * as it was to hear and understand the words.

Shakespeare was very busy at this time because he had decided to leave the King's Men and return to Stratford.

6
Return to Stratford

Shakespeare moved back to Stratford in 1610. There was only one thing about living outside London that he did not like: there were no plays or actors. Times had changed; the power and influence of the Puritans had spread, and plays were not allowed in the town. It was a pity, but Shakespeare had seen many plays and actors in his life, and he could still see them whenever he went to London. His break with London in 1610 was certainly not complete. He went there on business quite often. In fact, he had bought a house in Blackfriars not far from the theatre. For a fifty-year-old gentleman with a beautiful house, money, family, and friends both nearby and in London, life was very pleasant.

Shakespeare had enough memories for two lifetimes. He remembered the old Theatre and the new Globe, performances, earls, ladies, musicians, rebellions, punishments and Friday nights at the Mermaid tavern(a place to drink, eat and talk). On the first Friday of every month, a group of men used to meet to talk, drink, eat and laugh; Shakespeare, Ben Jonson, and many of the newer writers such as John Donne, Francis Beaumont and John Fletcher were there. Beaumont and Fletcher often worked

Ben Jonson

together and wrote some very popular plays. William Johnson, the owner of the Mermaid inn, was also a friend. He had helped Shakespeare to buy his London house. William Johnson sometimes got angry about the people who could think of nothing but religion. It is

Mr John Fletcher   Mr Francis Beaumont

recorded that in 1613 he was in trouble for serving meat instead of fish in his inn on a Friday.

Living in Stratford did not mean the end of writing for Shakespeare. Things were quieter now, but in the two or three years after leaving London he found that there were still plays to write. People wanted romances these days — Beaumont and Fletcher were good at writing those. *The Winter's Tale* was the first romance that Shakespeare wrote in Stratford. He liked it much better than *Pericles*, which he had not written alone.

If people wanted plays to help them forget everyday life, why not write a play about those islands in the warm Atlantic discovered by John Somers and the men from the *Sea Venture*? The survivors had said that the islands were magical. There were no people there, they said, but there were certainly spirits. That was an idea much too good to forget. Shakespeare turned the idea into one of his most successful and best-loved plays — *The Tempest*. It is a romance with a very special spiritual feeling about it, which makes it different to all his other romances and to all his other plays.

There was still one idea left in Shakespeare's mind from many years ago. He had never quite finished his group of history plays so that that they finished at the time of Elizabeth I, the queen of his young days. There was a good reason for this: history plays were not allowed during the times of the political trouble because they gave the people ideas about rebellion but now he had the time and the chance to finish the group of plays. He did not do it alone but wrote it with other writers in Stratford. At first they called the new history play *All is True*, but then the title was changed to *Henry VIII*. There are many good scenes in the play; in fact the individual scenes are more important than the story.

As far as we know, *Henry VIII* was the last of Shakespeare's plays, and it was certainly the end of the Globe Theatre: one of the best scenes in the play needed the sound of a big gun and it was this gun which set the Globe on fire. The company, including Shakespeare, were very brave and they built a second Globe Theatre. Although Shakespeare never acted there or wrote any plays for it, it was a successful theatre until 1642. (It was in that year that all the theatres were closed because the Puritans, led by Oliver Cromwell, took over the government of the country.)

In London, Ben Jonson was now the king of the playwrights. He was well known for his plays: *The Alchemist*,

Volpone and *Bartholomew Fair*, as well as for his many masques. Even he, however, had to keep his eye on the two new writers, Beaumont and Fletcher. It was probably Fletcher who worked with Shakespeare on *Henry VIII*.

The last years of Shakespeare's life were not very happy at home: his second daughter, Judith, married a man called Thomas Quiney. He was the owner of a tavern in Stratford and Shakespeare did not like him because he drank too much and spent too much money. Shakespeare probably wished that Judith had made a good marriage like her elder sister Susanna. She had married a local doctor called John Hall. Judith was thirty-one years old when she got married, which was quite late for a girl to marry at that time.

Shakespeare was so unhappy about the marriage that he left hardly any money in his will to Judith, or indeed to his own wife, Anne. He left most of his property to his favourite daughter Susanna, and only left his wife 'the second-best bed' from his house! Ten weeks after the marriage of Judith to Thomas Quiney, on 23rd April 1610, Shakespeare died.

There is a story that Ben Jonson and another writer friend came to see Shakespeare a few weeks before he died. They ate and drank a lot and enjoyed themselves very much, but Shakespeare caught a cold immediately afterwards and never recovered.

His wife Anne lived eight years longer and both his daughters had long lives. Susanna had no boys and Judith's sons all died young. It seemed as if fate had said that there should be no males to continue the Shakespeare name.

The name did not die, of course, it lived on in his writing. In a way, Shakespeare's name was born in the same year that his wife died. By 1623 only two actors (John Heminge and Henry Condell) remained of the original company of actors called The King's Men. (Richard Burbage had died in 1619). These two men had noticed how, in 1616, Ben Jonson had published his *Works*. They had seen how carefully he had watched over the printing and publishing of his writings. None of Shakespeare's plays had ever been published; a few of them had been printed by other people but some of the copies were so bad that they were nothing more than other people's remembered ideas about his plays.

Heminge and Condell collected the best copies of the plays and published them in one book. In the book there were thirty-six plays by Shakespeare, some poetry about him by Ben Jonson and others, a picture of him by Martin Droeshout and a list of the main actors in all the plays. About twenty of the plays had never been printed before. This book is now known as the *First Folio*.

It is strange to think that many of the people who knew Shakespeare, especially in Stratford, did not know the plays that he had written. It is even stranger to think that, without the *First Folio*, we, too, might never have heard of them. Shakespeare did not write the plays for us; he wrote them for the actors of his company, in his own time. Ben Jonson, John Heminge, and Henry Condell knew better; they could recognise great writing. Ben Jonson had exactly the right words: 'He was not of an age, but for all time.'

Mr. WILLIAM
SHAKESPEARES
COMEDIES,
HISTORIES, &
TRAGEDIES.

Published according to the True Originall Copies.

Martin Droeshout sculpsit London

LONDON
Printed by Isaac Iaggard, and Ed. Blount. 1623.

Exercises

Exercise 1

The three parts of these nine sentences are mixed up. Put the parts together so that the sentences agree with the story.

Example: The plague was a terrible illness. (**1** = 1*a*, 2*f*, 3*d*)

		1	2	3
1	*a*	**The plague**	forbade	performances inside the city walls.
2	*b*	Stratford Grammar School	poured	the first theatre in London
3	*c*	Shakespeare	showed	that the plague was a punishment from God.
4	*d*	The Mayor of London	thought	**a terrible illness**.
5	*e*	James Burbage	married	the problems of the country.
6	*f*	History plays	**was**	beer over the burning trousers.
7	*g*	The puritans	offered	the truest copies of Shakespeare's plays.
8	*h*	One of the audience	collected	Anne Hathaway in 1582.
9	*i*	Heminge and Condell	built	free education of certain boys.

Answers: See p. 56

Exercise 2

Put these words into their places in the text and copy out
the text.

1 both	8 performed	15 were
2 in	9 were	16 space
3 as	10 was	17 tavern
4 the	11 over	18 for
5 down	12 high	19 of
6 hole	13 first	20 a
7 and	14 by	

— theatres of Elizabeth I's time — the — proper theatre
buildings. Before the theatres — built, actors — plays in
market places, — yards, town halls or big rooms —
castles.

The stage was above ground level — could be seen by the
audience from — sides as well — from the front. In the
stage floor there was a covered — or trapdoor which went
— to a — below the stage. There was — smaller 'inner-
stage' at the back — the main stage. This was used — a
scene in a room or in a cave. There was also a place above
the stage. This was used — musicians or actors if the play
needed a mountain top, roof top or other — place. There
was a roof — the stage and above this there — another
space for stage machinery.

Answers: See p. 56

Exercise 3

These verbs are missed out of the text below.
Find their places and write out the full text.

were performed	was born
was performed	was drinking
would	went
was	was killed
wrote	got
had died	had

Christopher Marlowe the son of a shoemaker in
Canterbury. He on 6th February 1564, about two months
before William Shakespeare. He to King's School,
Canterbury and the University of Cambridge. He a BA
degree in 1584 and an MA degree in 1587. Also in 1587
his first play, Tamburlaine the Great. The main
characters in most of his tragedies, *Dr Faustus*, *The Jew of
Malta*, *Edward II* and others, by Edward Alleyn. It was
this actor that Marlowe in his mind when he wrote the
plays. In 1593 he with a knife at an inn in Deptford by the
man with whom he. If Shakespeare as young as Marlowe,
we probably now consider Marlowe as the greater playwright.

Answers: See p. 56

Exercise 4

Guided Compositions

Use the following notes with any information from the story. Write one or two paragraphs about the life-story of both these people.

Robert Greene
Born 1558, Norwich.
University degrees from Cambridge and Oxford.
Travelled much. Many friends among thieves and vagabonds.
Married 1583, one child, good wife.
Spent wife's money and went to London without family.
Lived with sister of famous thief, one son.
Became playwright.
Attacked most actors and several playwrights in writing.
Died after too much fish and wine 1592.

Anne Hathaway
One of large family. Born 1555.
Hathaway: common name in Warwickshire.
Father: Richard, farmer, died 1581.
Home: village of Shottery very near Stratford.
Married 1582. Child six months later.
Mother, Joan, died 1599.
Lived with husband's family.
Mentioned in husband's will.
Three children, including twins.

Exercise 5

Find out more about these subjects and write about them:

1 Twins.
2 The differences between plays and poetry in the sixteenth century.
3 Puritans and entertainment.
4 The social position of actors.
5 Bear-baiting.
6 Latin in sixteenth-century England.
7 Books published in the time of James I.
8 University education (the situation now compared to Shakespeare's day.)

Exercise 6

Quiz questions

1 Name a tragedy by Shakespeare about ancient Rome.
2 Who wrote *The Jew of Malta*?
3 What was the name of the church where William Shakespeare was given his name?
4 Name the four 'great' tragedies.
5 What was the job of Ben Jonson's father?
6 What colour of hair did Emilia Bassano have?
7 What was Henry Wriothesley's title?
8 In 1588, which ships were bigger, the Spanish or the English?

9 Name two of William's brothers.
10 In which English country is Stratford? (Look at a map of England.)
11 How many lines are there in a sonnet?
12 Name William Shakespeare's twin children.
13 What is the connection between Shakespeare and Bermuda?
14 Which play was being performed when the Globe burned down?
15 How did the Earl of Essex die?
16 What kind of play is *The Winter's Tale*?
17 What did Shakespeare leave to his wife in his will?
18 Who wrote: 'He was not of an age, but for all time'?
19 Name any three actors of the King's Men (apart from Shakespeare).
20 Name any three of the London theatres in Shakespeare's time.

Answers to Exercise 1 (p. 50)

1   1*a*, 2*f*, 3*d*.
2   1*b*, 2*g*, 3*i*.
3   1*c*, 2*e*, 3*h*.
4   1*d*, 2*a*, 3*a*.
5   1*e*, 2*i*, 3*b*.
6   1*f*, 2*c*, 3*e*.
7   1*g*, 2*d*, 3*c*.
8   1*h*, 2*b*, 3*f*.
9   1*i*, 2*h*, 3*g*.

Answers to Exercise 2 (p. 51)

Order of words as they should appear in the text:
4, 9, 13, 15, 8, 17, 2, 7, 1, 3, 6, 5, 16, 20, 19, 18, 14, 12, 11, 10.

Answers to Exercise 3 (p. 52)

Christoper Marlowe **was** the son of a shoemaker in Canterbury. He **was born** on 6th February 1564, about two months before William Shakespeare. He **went** to King's School, Canterbury and the University of Cambridge. He **got** a BA degree in 1584 and an MA degree in 1587. Also in 1587 his first play, *Tamburlaine the Great*, **was performed**. The main characters in most of his tragedies, *Doctor Faustus*, *The Jew of Malta*, *Edward II* and others, **were performed** by Edward Alleyn. It was this actor that Marlowe **had** in his mind when he **wrote** the plays. In 1593 he **was killed** with a knife at an inn in Deptford by the man with whom **he was drinking**. If Shakespeare **had died** as young as Marlowe, we **would** probably now consider Marlowe as the greater playwright of the two.

Glossary

(to) act   To speak as if you are someone else, in a play, for other people to see.

actor   A person who speaks in a play for others to see and enjoy.

admired   Liked and respected.

admiration   The feeling of liking and respect.

ancient   Very old; of times long ago.

art   The making of beautiful things e.g. paintings, books, music, etc.

audience   The crowd of people who watch a play or entertainment.

balcony   A place on the outside of a house from which there is a good view of the ground below.

bull-baiting   Making dogs fight a bull for entertainment.

burned down   Was destroyed by fire.

century   One hundred years. (The sixteenth century = the years 1501 to 1600).

certainly   Without doubt.

choice   The act of picking one thing one from several because it is the best.

citizen   A person, living in a town, who pays money to the local government.

coat of arms   A design used to represent a noble family, a town, a university etc.

comedy   A play about everyday life, amusing in parts and with a happy ending.

costume   Clothes, usually for a special purpose: the characters in a play wear costumes.

court   The public part of the home of a king or queen.

courteous   Very gentle and kind.

courtyard   The open area outside an inn, usually enclosed by a wall or buildings.

death   The end of life; the loss of life.

(to) discover   To find.

downfall   A fall from a high position in society to a low one.

drama   Plays for the public to see.

dramatic   Something is dramatic when it is acted or when it is full of excitement.

duty   Something good we feel that we have to do for someone else. For example, it is a child's duty to care for his parents when they are old.

earl   The title of a British nobleman; a member of the aristocracy.

education   The training or teaching received at school or university.

educated   Having received training or teaching at school or university.

elementary   First.

entertainment An event (play, song, dance etc.) which pleases the people who watch.

explode To burst; to blow up; to make a loud bang.

fashionable Popular at the moment.

frozen Turned to ice; solid; hard.

fruit An apple is the fruit of an apple tree.

genius Great power of the mind or imagination.

ghost The spirit of a dead person who appears as if they were still alive.

glove-making The trade of making gloves. Gloves are coverings which keep the hands warm, usually made of leather or wool.

grammar The rules of a language.

gratitude Thankfulness; appreciation; gratefulness.

horror Extreme terror, fear, or dislike.

identical An absolute likeness; exact sameness.

indoors Inside a building.

instrument A musical instrument is something which makes music eg. a trumpet, a drum etc.

justice fairness, rightness.

law The rules of a community.

lawyer A person who tells other people what the law is.

literature Books; the written language; works of art in writing.

magical Supernatural; mysterious; concerned with spirits.

military Of or for the army; concerned with soldiers; about war.

mind A person's intellectual powers, thoughts and reasoning.

misfortune Bad luck.

monarch King or queen of a country.

morality Morality plays were about people who were good or bad. They taught people about good and evil.

musician A person who makes music for others to hear.

(an) official Someone of authority or trust, usually employed in a public position.

(an) opportunity A good chance in life.

original First; earliest; not copied; not translated.

owner The person who has or possesses; the person to whom a thing belongs.

patriotic Feeling proud of your country.

patriotism The feeling of love and pride for your country.

patron Someone who helps another with money and kind words. A patron saint is a saint who is specially connected with a certain country.

perform To do something (e.g. a song, a dance) for people to see and enjoy.

performance A song, a dance, or a play which is done for people to see and enjoy.

(to) persecute To make someone suffer because of what they believe.

plague A deadly illness which spreads quickly and is carried by rats.

plays Stories acted by people on a stage for other people to see. They are usually about three hours long.

playwright Someone who writes plays.

poem An idea in words which are put together in a special form which is beautiful or interesting.

poetry Poems: the art of creating beauty with words.

political Of the public affairs of a government or nation.

pride A feeling of happiness about something: pleasure.

printer A man who puts words onto paper and makes books.

prison A place where a person is kept locked up against his will, by law.

professional Practising a skill to earn a living.

property Things owned; possessions; belonging to someone.

protect To keep from danger, to keep safe.

provinces Any part of the country outside London.

publish To print a book in order to sell copies

punishment Pain given to someone who has done something wrong, e.g. going to prison is a punishment for breaking the law.

qualities Kindness is a good quality. Evil is a bad quality.

rebel A person who fights the government, or refuses to be loyal to it.

rebellion The act of fighting against the government, or refusing to obey it.

religious Of religion; holy; concerned with God.

respectable Worthy of respect; approved of by society.

romance A story with characters and scenes far from everyday life; a fictitious and wonderful tale.

Roman Of ancient Rome.

saint See *patron saint*.

scenery   The painted background used on the stage of a theatre.

seeds   The beginning. A plant begins as a seed and grows until it shows a flower or fruit.

sown   Started to grow.

spite   In spite of means: not prevented by.

spy   A person who tries to get secret information, usually about the political or military affairs of other countries.

stage   A raised platform or floor on which plays are performed.

struggles   Difficulties, battles.

style   A way of doing things.

suffer   To feel pain, grief, loss or punishment.

sword   A weapon with a cutting edge and a sharp point.

talent   Natural gifts; a special ability to do something.

throne   The king or queen's position.

tolerant   Patient, letting other people do what they want to.

torture   Deliberate and severe pain given to someone.

tragedy   A play with a serious or sad story and an unhappy ending.

translation   The meaning of a piece of writing in one language expressed in another language.

triangle   A figure to form with three angles and three sides; a love-affair involving three people.   △

twins   Two children born at the same time of the same mother.

university   A place of higher education.

victory   Success in a battle or war.

violence Physical force (usually used by a human being); brutality.

violent Using great physical force or brutality.

visual To be seen.

wisdom You have wisdom if you know a lot and if you are very good.